I0605366

CREATIVE CAREERS

Creative Careers in the

FASHION INDUSTRY

Stuart A. Kallen

San Diego, CA

Printed in the United States

For more information, contact:
ReferencePoint Press, Inc.
PO Box 27779
San Diego, CA 92198
www.ReferencePointPress.com

LIBRARY OF CONGRESS CATALOGING-IN-PUBLICATION DATA

Author: Stuart A. Kallen
Title: Creative Carees in the Fashion Industry
Description: San Diego, CA : ReferencePoint Press, 2026. | Series: Creative Careers
Includes bibliographical references and index
Identifiers: LCCN 2025003012 (print) | ISBN 9781678210243 library binding | ISBN 9781678210250 ebook

For compete cataloging-in-publication data please go to www.loc.gov.

Contents

Introduction: Fashioning a Career

The fashion industry has long attracted a diverse group of trendsetters, designers, and other creatives whose artistic vision is centered on clothing, shoes, and accessories. Many are inspired by stories of individuals with unique talents and an eye for style who have started small and worked their way up to the top of the industry. Fashion icon Ralph Lauren, for example, began his career as a sales assistant at a Brooks Brothers store in New York City. Lauren left the job to work as a necktie salesman for several years before designing and producing his own line of neckties. He founded the Ralph Lauren Corporation at age twenty-eight and launched the Polo brand of menswear soon after. In 2011 Lauren explained his fashion design philosophy: "You have to create something from nothing."[1] In 2024 Lauren's luxury fashion empire generated more than $7 billion a year.

Most career opportunities in the fashion industry do not involve becoming a household name by creating something from nothing, but many have made a good living and advanced in their fields. The global apparel market is populated by specialists who focus on textile design, product development, clothing and accessory production, fashion marketing, fashion journalism, makeup and hairstyling, retail sales, and inventory management. Some of the jobs are filled by fashion institute graduates or people with a degree from a college. Other jobs are taken by those who started as minimum wage workers. Janet Francis, an executive at UGG footwear, says she started her career in high school working on the sales floor of a department store. She went on to become a buyer, then a visual merchandiser, a professional who creates appealing displays in stores. Francis eventually worked her way up to a senior account executive. "As you can see my entire career started in retail," Francis says. "This gave me the skills I needed to learn the fashion industry and I'm so happy I did!"[2]

The Business of Fashion

The fashion industry is highly competitive, and many who pursue careers in this sector do not earn huge salaries. But fashion is also a career that an artistic amateur can literally start at home with little more than a sewing machine, some cloth, and a dream of success. This is the path followed by fashion designer and businesswoman Tory Burch. In 2004 Burch designed the first pieces of her successful sportswear brand TRB on her kitchen table.

While success stories form part of the glitz of the industry, the fashion world is about much more than glamour, glitterati, and runway shows. Superstar designers might attract the most attention, but the $1.8 trillion industry is driven at the most basic level by those who make and sell products. Fashion industry professionals focus on consumer trends, product development, pricing, manufacturing, and other aspects of retail sales. That is even true for self-employed designers who market their wares on e-commerce sites like Etsy and Amazon Handmade. Successful freelance designers draw up business plans that detail social media promotions, market analysis, financial projections, and sales strategies.

People often say designers like Lauren and Burch had overnight success, but they know there is no such thing. Most successful people in the fashion industry first work low-wage jobs while gaining hands-on experience. The lessons learned provide valuable insight for those who go on to build a fashion empire.

The fashion industry is fast paced, competitive, and unpredictable. It is also a highly desirable industry, and finding a place within it can be a challenge. Experienced professionals recommend working in numerous sectors of the industry to determine where one fits in. Those interested should try their hands at designing and producing fashions, promoting and marketing them online, networking with others in the business, attending a fashion institute, and taking on part-time jobs or internships in the industry. If that sounds like a lot of hard work, it is. But those with the talent to innovate and adjust to ever-changing trends can thrive and find success. As Burch said in 2024, "You have to have conviction and a vision and not deviate from that, but also be able to move into the current. It's so important to have a unique point of view and make your mark and do something that is answering a need, but also be able to move when you have to move in different directions."[3]

What Does a Fashion Photographer Do?

Millions of people with smartphones think of themselves as photographers, and social media is overflowing with tens of billions of their photographs. But fashion photographers do more than point and click with their phones. Most professional fashion photographers take photos with complex cameras that can cost $5,000 or more. The photographers usually work with lighting kits that include high-powered lamps, light stands, booms, and reflectors.

At a Glance

Number of Jobs
151,100 in 2023*

Pay
$40,760 in 2023*

Educational Requirements
High school diploma or equivalent

Personal Qualities
Artistic, self-motivated, computer skills

Working Conditions
Full or part time in offices and studios; some travel and long hours when deadlines loom

Future Job Outlook
Growth of 4 percent through 2033*

* For all photographers

Fashion photographers take photos of clothing, shoes, and accessories arranged in tasteful displays or worn by models. Before a shoot the photographers examine fabrics and clothing textures to see how they reflect light. They take test shots and adjust camera settings. They use tools like light meters to read exposure levels and color temperature gauges to ensure whites and colors appear natural. During a shoot a fashion photographer will choose from a variety of lenses. Standard lenses are used for basic shots, wide angle lenses take in a wide field of view, and zoom lenses allow the

Capturing a Creative Vision

"I want to tell people and encourage photographers that it's not about how technical you are. It's about what you see and it's about pushing that button at the right time. Don't get lost in the technical side of being a photographer because it steals your vision away. You want to be creative. It's important to know how to expose and set the camera right, but it's really, really important to not get so caught up in the technical. Be in the moment with everything."

—Jim Jordan, fashion photographer

Quoted in Taya Iv, "Interview with Jim Jordan," Great Big Photography World, February 29, 2024. https://greatbigphotographyworld.com.

photographer to frame the shot from a distance or zoom in for a close-up. The fish-eye lens, which creates a circular panoramic image, might be used for a special effect. After photo shoots are finished, fashion photographers manipulate raw photos with image processing software like Adobe Photoshop or Lightroom.

In addition to technical skills, fashion photographers draw on their artistic talents to create eye-catching images suitable for glossy fashion magazines and online ads. Fashion photographers understand how to frame shots to best highlight garments and models. They might employ props ranging from flowers to live animals, which are meant to provide an attention-grabbing element to a photo. All are used to create an alluring story within a photograph. Fashion photographer Mark Delong explains, "Good fashion photography captures a moment in another world, filled with its own characters and settings. Without a good story, an image is flat and shallow—a compelling narrative gives a photograph depth, interest, and vitality."[4]

While a good understating of the technical and artistic aspects of photography is important, fashion photographers need to develop a good working relationship with models. In films and

TV shows, fashion photographers are often parodied as egotists yelling commands at flustered models. But as fashion photographer Kait Robinson states:

> I simply try to make the [model] feel as comfortable as possible. And I'm talking about from the moment they enter through the door. When the time comes to shoot, it makes both of our jobs much easier because we've already "broken the ice" in a way. I don't particularly like fashion shots that are obviously pose-y, so making the subject comfortable lends itself to that casual, cool vibe which I much prefer.[5]

Models are not the only people who need to feel comfortable. Fashion shoots have many moving parts, and photographers often work as executive producers. They hire models, digital technicians, wardrobe stylists, hairstylists, makeup artists, prop stylists, and others. They oversee budgets and set schedules for the numerous tasks that occur before, during, and after a photoshoot.

How Do You Become a Fashion Photographer?

Education and Training

A college degree is not necessary for those who dream of becoming a fashion photographer. However, photographers who wish to improve their skills and employment prospects take photography classes at universities, vocational institutes, or trade schools. Courses teach the basics, including equipment, processes, and photographic methods. Some seek a bachelor's degree in photography, fine art, or related business fields like fashion design or fashion merchandising.

Most successful fashion photographers say that they began pursuing their art at an early age. Robinson—who has worked for clients such as Louis Vuitton, Dior, Chloé, and Givenchy—says her love of great photos prompted her to take photography classes in high school. Early on, Robinson learned traditional photography techniques, including shooting and developing film and printing photos in a darkroom. She also developed a love of fashion and style in high school. This led her to set up amateur fashion shoots with her friends, focusing on clothing, hair, and makeup. In college Robinson studied advertising for a time before dropping out to attend the Fashion Institute of Technology in New York City, where she earned a bachelor of fine arts in photography.

Fashion photographer Jim Jordan—who shoots photo spreads for clients such as Bentley, Rolex, and American Express—also started his career in high school. Jordan began working as a hair and makeup artist in Los Angeles at age fifteen. He photographed the models he worked with but remained a stylist for twelve years before an executive at J. Crew saw his photographs and hired him for a two-week shoot in Hawaii, thus launching his career. Since that time Jordan's fashion photos have appeared in *Vogue*, *Harper's Bazaar*, *GQ*, and other prestigious publications.

Skills and Personality

Most fashion photographers enjoy educating themselves about their craft. They read about the history of fashion photography and the industry and study the work of renowned fashion photographers like Helmut Newton, Annie Leibovitz, and Richard Avedon. Robinson, who earned worldwide recognition in her early twenties, describes her path to self-education: "When I was around 16 years old and just getting into photography, a family member gave me a book on the basics. I read it front to back probably six times in a week's span. I think having both an appreciation for the technicality as well as the aesthetics really pushed me to want to photograph."[6]

Successful fashion photographers also have a good head for business. They manage production budgets with an eye to keep-

A model poses for a photographer during a fashion shoot. The photographer uses lighting and various poses to convey a sense of fun—a feeling that is aimed at increasing brand appeal.

ing costs as low as possible. Fashion photographers might also oversee travel budgets and pay rates for crew members.

On the Job

Employers

The Bureau of Labor Statistics (BLS) says that around two-thirds of all professional photographers are self-employed. This figure also applies to those who work in the fashion industry, according to the career advice website Vault. Other fashion photographers work for fashion design firms, advertising agencies, large retail stores, and print or online media.

Freelance fashion photographers usually obtain work on the basis of their portfolios. These online photo collections highlight a photographer's most impactful shots from their most notable assignments. The photos are usually posted to personal websites

Setting the Scene

"The key to professional fashion photography is showcasing the pieces without letting the clothing overwhelm the environment. The same goes for the backdrop, it should complement the styles you're shooting and not distract. The job of the model and the location is to draw attention to the clothing, in a nutshell. The entire image should convey a distinct feeling of time and place, in a world that lives beyond the photograph. In [one shoot] we chose locations that not only complimented the color of the styles, but also set them within a scene, a world that the viewer can easily buy into."

—Tory Smith, fashion, beauty, and advertising photographer

Tory Smith, "Storytelling as a Freelance eCommerce Photographer," Tory Smith, December 4, 2021. https://tory-smith.com/storytelling-as-a-freelance-ecommerce-photographer.

and social media sites. Freelancers regularly update their portfolios, websites, and social media feeds. They rely on hashtags to attract potential clients. "Think of hashtags as a pipeline to the rest of the world," freelance photographer Allen Harper writes. "Every tag you use acts [as] a connection with other users. If you use 5, there are 5 outlets that others can use to view your image. If you use 30, now you have 30 outlets."[7]

Working Conditions

Fashion photographers work in offices and studios full time or part time. Hours vary depending on deadlines and other specifics of an assignment. The job might involve traveling to various locations and working long hours while shooting photos in outdoor settings like beaches, parks, or gardens. Fashion photography can also be seasonal, with a heavy schedule leading up to and through what is called Fashion Week. This seven-day event takes place every February and September and involves designers presenting their latest fashions at runway shows in New York, London, Paris, and Milan, Italy.

Earnings and Advancement

The BLS says the average annual salary for all photographers in 2023 was $40,760. But fashion photographers earn more money than those who work weddings, commercials, and other photography assignments. According to the employment website Salary.com, fashion photographers earned a median annual income of $65,511 in 2024.

Those just beginning their fashion photography careers as freelancers can expect to earn less than average. However, self-employed fashion photographers can advance their careers and boost their incomes in other ways. Some offer photography courses on educational websites and in tutorial videos. Those with many followers on social media can become influencers who earn income by promoting cameras and other tools of the fashion photography trade. Successful fashion photographers enhance their earnings by branching out into related sectors. For example, Jordan runs a talent agency called White Cross that manages models, actors, and musical acts.

What Is the Future Outlook for Fashion Photographers?

The BLS says employment for all photographers is expected to grow by 4 percent through 2033. But some analysts say employment opportunities for fashion photographers will grow faster as the highly competitive fashion industry seeks to promote the latest trends on social media. As fashion photographer Nick Harington points out, "Social media platforms, powered by fashion photography, have given a voice to diverse fashion influencers who challenge traditional norms and showcase alternative perspectives on style."[8]

Find Out More

American Society of Media Photographers (ASMP)

www.asmp.org

The ASMP hosts seminars and provides news articles and videos related to media photography. The society's website provides a platform for photographers to showcase their work and helps members connect with clients. It also has a bridge program for students interested in photography.

Professional Photographers of America (PPA)

www.ppa.com

This nonprofit organization provides professional development, webinars, tutorials, and free courses that focus on various photography niches. The PPA also publishes *Professional Photographer* magazine.

University Photographers' Association of America (UPAA)

https://upaa.org

The UPAA is an organization of college and university photographers. The association hosts symposiums and contests and publishes blogs, job listings, and *Contact Sheet* magazine.

What Does a Fashion Stylist Do?

The annual Met Gala is one of the biggest nights of the year for the fashion industry. The fundraising event for the Metropolitan Museum of Art in New York City brings together around two hundred A-list celebrities. Many attendees wear over-the-top outfits that attract widespread attention. In 2024 social media was abuzz when singer and actress Zendaya wore a light-up Cinderella dress, and singer Rihanna walked the red carpet in a 16-foot (4.9 m) golden cape. While the media focused on the flamboyant fashionistas, the fashion stylists who put together the iconic looks rarely received mention. But Zendaya's fashion stylist, Law Roach, and Rhianna's stylist, Jahleel Weaver, are well-known luminaries widely celebrated in the world of fashion.

Fashion stylist is one of the most coveted job titles in the fashion industry. Those who work as fashion stylists curate complete outfits down to the smallest details. They provide clients with unique looks for daily wear, runway shows, fashion photoshoots, and star-studded events like the Academy Awards and the Met Gala.

At a Glance

Number of Jobs
13,031 in 2024

Pay
$45,524 in 2024

Educational Requirements
None

Personal Qualities
Expert in style, knowledge of fashion and trends, self-motivated, good research skills, computer skills

Working Conditions
Full or part time in offices, studios, and showrooms; some travel

Future Job Outlook
Growth of 3 percent through 2029

Fashion stylist Law Roach poses in 2022 with one of his famous clients, singer-actress Zendaya. Fashion stylists like Roach create unique looks for their clients—for daily wear as well as for star-studded events like the Academy Awards and Met Gala.

Sometimes known as image consultants, fashion stylists work with actors, musicians, wealthy individuals, businesspeople, and politicians to select trendy clothes that complement their client's body type and lifestyle. As Zadrian Smith says about his celebrity clients, who include model Winnie Harlow and actress Ariana DeBose, "We want to understand what they like, what they don't like, what colors they like and what silhouettes they like. And once we have that information, it's up to us to take our years of experience and our expertise and kind of put that all into a melting pot and make it come together."[9]

Fashion stylists source clothing and accessories from designers in New York, Los Angeles, Paris, Milan, and other fashion capitals. They shop for garments, shoes, and accessories. Sometimes stylists borrow items for a single event from a famous designer, ensuring borrowed items are returned in perfect condition after they are worn. Those designers hope to reap rewards after their items are showcased in photoshoots or at a red-carpet event.

Some fashion stylists are specialists. Those who work with individuals are known as personal stylists. E-commerce stylists specialize in curating clothing for online retailers. These stylists highlight appealing fashions that are meant to entice customers to hit the "Add to cart" button. Photoshoot stylists, as the name implies, work with fashion photographers. They dress models, celebrities, and others at photoshoots. Runway stylists provide their services at fashion shows, choosing accessories, shoes, and other items that best show off the clothing worn by models. Wardrobe stylists, also called film/TV stylists, specialize in dressing actors in styles that fit specific historic periods, situations, or settings.

How Do You Become a Fashion Stylist?

Education and Training

A college education is not necessary to become a fashion stylist, but those who attend a fashion institute can gain valuable insight into the fashion industry. Students learn the professional vocabulary used in the fashion business and study numerous styling genres, such as casual wear, high fashion, streetwear, gothic, and minimalist. Fashion institutes are great places to network and build a portfolio of work, often referred to as a lookbook, that can be used after graduation to attract attention and land gigs.

Prospective fashion stylists do not have to wait to attend an institute of higher learning to begin building careers. Most develop a love for clothing and styling at an early age. Stylist Kate Young, whose celebrity clients include Selena Gomez, Michelle Williams, and Dakota Johnson, was obsessed with fashion as a young girl. She would often visit the library, where she could pore over fashion magazines and absorb the latest trends. Young majored in English in college but was lucky enough to land a job as an assistant to Anna Wintour, the legendary editor of *Vogue* magazine. In 2003 Young was picked to style singer Gwen Stefani for the first cover of *Teen Vogue*. This led her to a career as a successful freelance stylist. Young explains how she learned her trade: "So much of what I did as an assistant was keep a notebook and write down everything all of the editors and photographers said that I didn't know. I didn't know the movie references. I didn't know the art references. You have to research it and figure out what you like. Read articles with people you admire, and when they say a name you don't know, go down that hole and figure it out."[10]

Law Roach's love of fashion led him on a different path. He opened a vintage clothing boutique in Chicago in 2009. By chance, Kanye West visited and bought some clothes. Then, Roach says, "[the store] just kind of exploded. We started to get calls from stylists around the world in London, Milan, New York, and L.A. asking for things. I just started saying I was a stylist. I don't know if I knew a lot about fashion, but I knew about style, because style is what you're born with."[11] Roach said he enhances his career prospects by watching YouTube tutorials and reading through dozens of fashion magazines going back to the 1970s.

Internships

Celebrity stylist Basia Richard says most fashion stylists begin their careers by working as interns. This helps them meet clients and garner recommendations. "A lot of this industry works by recommendations," says Richard, who started out as an intern herself. "Intern for a stylist, become their assistant. The key is to

Looks, Ideas, and Visions

"I start with the conversation with the client. How they're feeling in that time. Sometimes that's a nod to their character from the show or film they're promoting or it can be just a feeling. From there my mind normally whirls with ideas and visions. Then me and my wonderful assistant . . . reach out to the designers and ask if they're able to lend. Sometimes they can't. . . . There are lots of factors you have to navigate your way around until you find the options that fit your vision. Once we've 'called in' lots of looks from designers we'll do a fitting in my studio."

—Aimee Croysdill, fashion stylist

Quoted in Barbour, "Spring-Summer Styling with Aimee Croysdill: Q&A," February 24, 2024. www.barbour.com.

develop a relationship with these stylists so they can recommend you. . . . Internships teach you how to start a job, how to finish the job, how to go from the show room to costume houses."[12] Internships also help prospective stylists build their portfolios.

Skills and Personality

Fashion stylists need to be creative to build looks that are unique and stand out in a crowd. But creativity is built on strong research skills. Successful fashion stylists spend hours online studying the latest trends, researching different looks, learning about their client's favorite styles, and sourcing the garments they need. Stylists also rely on computer skills to plan events, keep appointments, and line up their next gigs.

Fashion stylists need to maintain a positive attitude under circumstances that can be trying at times. Richard says, "As a celebrity stylist you will be working with lots of different personalities and fashion tastes. So you want to make everyone happy and make them comfortable."[13]

Know Yourself and Your Tastes

"My advice to young stylists is first and foremost understand and know authentically who you are as a person. Understand what you love and what your tastes are, and once you are secure in that, share that with your potential clients. And if they love that, then that's a great match. And if they don't, that's not a good match. And there's nothing wrong with that. You're not gonna be for everyone. Everyone's not your client."

—Zadrian Smith, fashion stylist

Quoted in Janelle Sessoms, "How Zadrian Smith Went from Trained Dancer to A-List Celebrity Stylist," Fashionista, February 7, 2024. https://fashionista.com.

Like all fashion professionals, stylists need to understand business accounting practices. Most are assigned a budget for each project. As journalist Kristen Swain explains:

> Sometimes the budget given the stylist is large for just a few pieces, other times it can be very tight for a large variety of clothing. Regardless of what the budget is, the stylist must be able to stay within its confines when shopping. As a stylist, when you go over budget you risk losing your client and—because stylists often purchase items themselves and then are reimbursed by the client—harming yourself financially.[14]

On the Job

Employers

Most fashion stylists are freelancers who established a client base working in the fashion industry as an assistant, buyer, photographer, or hair and makeup artist. Freelance fashion stylists often have personal websites featuring blogs and lookbooks, and they also promote themselves on social media sites like Instagram. Some personal stylists are employed full time by celebrities and wealthy clients. Fashion stylists also work full time for retail fashion brands, e-commerce sites, and fashion magazines.

Working Conditions

A fashion stylist's hours can be long and irregular. Freelancers might work from a home office but travel regularly to attend runway shows, visit brand showrooms, and conduct personal shopping trips for clients. The work of a fashion stylist can be stressful. Busy fashion stylists often juggle several short-term projects at once. Celebrities who are used to having everything their own way can be temperamental. Runway shows are high-pressure events in which every look needs to be perfect. In the highly competitive fashion industry, mistakes can be disastrous. Swain writes, "If a stylist can't meet the client's expectations, she may lose a job or paying client as well as a reference to the client's personal and professional contacts."[15]

Earnings and Advancement

The employment website Zippia says fashion stylists earned an average annual income of $45,524 in 2024. However, fashion stylists with high levels of experience and expertise who live in New York, Los Angeles, and other fashion capitals can expect to earn more. Those at the top of their game, like Roach and Weaver, can earn millions by branching out with their own clothing and cosmetic lines.

What Is the Future Outlook for Fashion Stylists?

Zippia maintains that the demand for fashion stylists is expected to grow by 3 percent by 2029, slightly below the average job growth of 4 percent for all jobs. While celebrities and others will continue to rely on fashion stylists for their unique looks, there is a limited number of new openings in the upper echelons of the fashion world.

Find Out More

Costume Society of America (CSA)

www.costumesocietyamerica.com

The CSA focuses on the past, present, and future of clothing and fashion. The society hosts national symposia, publishes *Dress* magazine, and provides grants and awards to members.

Fashion Guild

www.thefashionguild.com

The Fashion Guild is a community resource for freelance fashion stylists. It hosts events and provides job resources, business advice, and online training courses for fashion stylists and others in the industry.

International Fashion Jewelry and Accessory Group

https://ifjag.com

The International Fashion Jewelry and Accessory Group is a member-owned association made up of designers and producers of fashion jewelry and accessories. Its website displays the latest in trendsetting products.

What Does a Retail Buyer Do?

Some people prefer to purchase their fashions on e-commerce websites. Others like to browse in clothing stores, where they can try on a wide range of garments. Whatever a shopper's preferences, most of the available clothing and accessories have been selected by retail buyers. These professionals, also known as fashion buyers or purchasing agents, are responsible for purchasing large quantities of products wholesale from clothing and accessory manufacturers. The fashions are then sold to individual customers at retail stores or on e-commerce platforms.

Retail buyers have a keen sense of fashion and an eye for the latest trends. They follow fashion blogs, read fashion magazines, and scroll through social media platforms, like TikTok and Instagram, to learn about the most promising new designers and latest fashion trends. Buyers conduct market research and analyze sales data from the recent past to determine consumer preferences, which can change rapidly in the fast-paced fashion world. They study the fashion lines offered by competitors and read customer

At a Glance

Number of Jobs
605,400 in 2023*

Pay
$77,180 in 2023*

Educational Requirements
Bachelor's degree in fashion merchandising, design, marketing, or related field

Personal Qualities
Eye for fashion; well organized; good math, business, and research skills

Working Conditions
Full time in offices, with considerable travel

Future Job Outlook
Growth of 7 percent through 2033*

* Includes buyers in a variety of fields

reviews and feedback of various products on e-commerce sites. Katie Guest, associate buyer for Timberland, explains the importance of market research: "In order to create a revenue driving product, it's important for you to collect selling history. One of my 'ah ha' moments was when I stopped thinking of what I personally liked and started analyzing the top revenue driving product. What common themes are in these products, is there a way to blend the top styles together? . . . This is the fun part of the job."[16]

After conducting research, retail buyers contact designers and suppliers in person, by phone, or in video calls. Buyers often visit a vendor's fashion showroom or production plant to view the latest offerings. Fashions are closely inspected for quality and fit. Garments and accessories are photographed for later reference. When this process is completed, buyers negotiate prices for pieces they have selected and sign purchase orders based on a careful analysis of consumer preferences.

Most retail buyers regularly attend apparel trade shows held in New York City, Los Angeles, and other fashion capitals around the globe. These events, which allow buyers to meet designers, browse the latest collections, and source suppliers, attract upward of twenty thousand attendees from all sectors of the fashion world. A fashion buyer known as Ariane says this is her least favorite part of her job. "Just imagine having to go through this entire process of long hours, jetlag, tight deadlines, non-stop running," she relates. "Just think about doing this 6 times per year. It certainly is one of the most exhausting jobs inside the fashion industry."[17]

In addition to the work of purchasing clothing lines, retail buyers attend meetings with sales teams, marketers, store managers, accounting personnel, and executives in which they set retail prices and develop sales strategies.

Administrative tasks for retail buyers include using spreadsheet software such as Microsoft Excel to track and analyze budgets, sales, returns, inventories, and other data. Ariane says she would not call her job glamorous, but she admits, "I have to say it's pretty awesome being able to see the collections before anyone else and there is nothing more rewarding than selling all the products I selected and purchased. . . . When I see our clients being so happy for what we chose for them, it's all worth it."[18]

How Do You Become a Retail Buyer?

Education and Training

Employers usually expect retail buyers to have a bachelor's degree. Those who earn a bachelor's in fashion merchandising learn about product development, accounting practices, and manufacturing processes. A bachelor's degree in marketing focuses on advertising, retail sales, brand management, and public relations. Those who pursue a bachelor's degree in fashion design learn about the fashion industry, garment design and construction, and illustration. Some companies, such as Bealls Outlet, have buyer training programs for qualified candidates.

Like many in the fashion industry, retail buyers tend to be lifelong lovers of clothing and fashion. In 2023 a blogger known as Ivonne described how she became a buyer for the clothing retailer Ross Dress for Less:

> My family was really poor when I was younger. . . . I would always get hand-me-down clothes from my older cousins. . . . When junior high came around, I taught myself how to sew and would make clothes with the leftover fabric from my mom's sewing job. And as I got older, I knew I wanted to work in fashion. I am 27 now and have been in buying since I've graduated college.[19]

Internships

Ivonne says she initially wanted to work in fashion public relations and marketing, but she landed a paid internship as a buyer at

Ross. She enjoyed the work and was hired by the company after she graduated. Based on her experience, Ivonne offers this advice to prospective retail buyers: "INTERN! That is the best way to find out if this is the job for you. I know many aspiring buyers that interned for this and did NOT like it. They went to school studying and training for this role and end up completely hating what buyers actually do. And honestly, if you love fashion, intern in any position to test the waters."[20]

Skills and Personality

Retail buyers of fashion combine creative vision with business skills. Fashion buyers need to appreciate the art and style of clothing, but they must also understand sales data and the mathematics of profit and loss. Brigitte Chartrand, a retail buyer at Ssense, says, "One of the top qualities we look for are analytical skills. We are such a data-driven company that selecting the right products is only a portion of the work that we do; analyzing data is a greater part of the job. And of course, your sense of style and ability to spot trends is paramount."[21]

Buyers need strong negotiating skills to obtain the best prices from vendors. This requires a talent for communicating with producers, which can lead to early access to exclusive lines. Communication skills across languages and cultures are also a plus, according to fabric buyer Karen Lott. "[Every morning] I have 60 e-mails from vendors in Turkey, Italy, Hong Kong, Hungary or even nearby in New York City," she says. "The e-mails usually contain information about fabric delivery and financing. . . . For our [South] Korean suppliers, we have to show proof of payment before they export. All Korean orders have to have a Korean insurance agency."[22]

Good research skills are important for retail buyers, who need a strong basis for predicting consumer tastes. Ariane explains, "As a buyer I am constantly asking myself 'What were the best sellers from last season and what is going to be the next big

Building Skills as an Intern

"The experience I gained during my internship with Primark was invaluable. I was working alongside the women's sportswear team and learned so much from them. During the six weeks, I was shadowing the trainee buyer on the team. Every Monday we would attend trade meetings discussing the sales of our products from the previous week. We would attend fit sessions with products that were being developed and would issue comments and changes that had to be made to the supplier. . . . Once everyone was happy with a product we then would email the supplier to let them know that the product had been approved and they could begin production."

—Lorna Skelly, fashion buyer intern

Quoted in Portobello Institute, "Lorna Skelly—Fashion Buying Internship to Dream Job," 2024. https://portobelloinstitute.com.

trend?' There are times when you see things you never thought people would actually buy, but then they end up sold out and a customers' favorite."[23]

On the Job

Employers

Walk through any shopping mall and you will see businesses that employ retail buyers. Some work for large department stores like Macy's, Nordstrom, and Saks Fifth Avenue; others work for single-brand stores like Gucci, Ann Taylor, and Abercrombie & Fitch. Retail buyers who specialize in fashion also purchase clothing and accessories for discount stores like Target and Walmart that sell a wide range of merchandise. Some retail buyers work for e-commerce sites such as Shein, Zara, and JD.com.

Planning and People Skills

"A buyer needs good organizational and planning skills. And people skills because you need the store employees to execute on your directions. . . . Retail is fast-paced which can be exciting because there's always something new to work on, but there's also pressure because sales revenue is directly related to how well a buyer executes their job. Keep in mind that many retailers have consolidated buying positions to one central corporate location, so you might need to move in order to find a position. Experience working in retail will help you with positioning for opportunities and for making certain you enjoy that type of working environment."

—Ann Newman, sales associate

Ann Newman, "What Does a Typical Day Look like for a Wholesale & Retail Buyer?," Career Village, May 14, 2023. www.careervillage.org.

Working Conditions

Retail buyers work full time in offices, and they often travel to trade shows, showrooms, warehouses, and factories where clothes and accessories are made. Most retail buyers do not have large travel budgets, and accommodations are seldom luxurious. Retail buyers often say the best part of the job comes after the workday is finished. Buyers attend evening launch parties and other events where they network and meet colleagues in a relaxed atmosphere.

Earnings and Advancement

The Bureau of Labor Statistics (BLS) groups retail buyers in a category that includes non-fashion buyers such as purchasing managers and purchasing agents, who work in a wide range of industries from government agencies to manufacturers. The median annual salary was $77,180 in 2023 for all workers in these sectors. People who are employed as retail fashion buyers often begin their careers on the retail floor, in assistant buyer positions, or in some other aspect of the fashion retail industry.

What Is the Future Outlook for Retail Buyers?

The BLS says employment for all buyers and purchasing agents and managers is expected to grow by 7 percent through 2033. Marketing analysts say growth for fashion buyers will likely be more rapid in the e-commerce sector as consumers continue to drift away from malls in favor of shopping online.

Find Out More

American Purchasing Society (APS)

www.american-purchasing.com
The APS is made up of buyers, purchasing managers, and other purchasing professionals. The APS website provides books, seminars, courses, job listings, and access to *Professional Purchasing* monthly magazine.

National Retail Federation (NRF)

https://nrf.com
This organization is the world's largest retail trade association. The NRF provides a jobs board, courses, and work opportunities to those who are pursuing careers in retail. The NRF Foundation Campus offers scholarships and provides information about internships.

Next Level Purchasing Association (NLPA)

www.certitrek.com/nlpa
The NLPA is an educational organization that offers online courses, coaching, blogs, white papers, and certification programs to retail buyers and other procurement specialists.

What Does a Fashion Designer Do?

Fashion designer Caroline Zimbalist thinks of herself as a traditional artist. Zimbalist likes to defy boundaries with her work and explore new ways of using unconventional materials. This led Zimbalist to create a distinctive fashion line. She melds natural fabrics like cotton, silk, and wool with bioplastics—plastics made from biodegradable materials like gelatin and cornstarch. Zimbalist says each of her fantastical, hand-painted creations is "like a painting coming off the wall and wrapping around a body."[24]

At a Glance

Number of Jobs
21,900 in 2023

Pay
$79,290 in 2023

Educational Requirements
Bachelor's degree in fashion design or fashion merchandising

Personal Qualities
Artistic, sewing talents, business skills, good communication skills

Working Conditions
Full or part time in offices, sewing rooms, photo studios, and at fashion shows

Future Job Outlook
Growth of 5 percent through 2033

Zimbalist is a freelancer whose unique designs stand out in the crowded world of fashion. This helped her build a brand that has attracted superstar clients, including singer Chappell Roan. Countless lovers of art, fashion, and design dream of launching a career like Zimbalist's. But the odds against becoming a superstar fashion designer are about 160,000 to 1, according to a ten-year study by the Princeton Review. And fashion designers like Donna Karan and Betsey Johnson who become household names are not just lucky—they work incredibly hard to follow consumer trends while staying one step ahead of the competition.

The hit reality TV show *Project Runway*, which began its twenty-first season in 2025, provides a window into the lives of fashion designers. Most of the contestants on the show are freelancers. To get a chance to compete, designers must wow the judges with impressive pieces from their fashion collections. Once they are accepted to appear on the show, the contestants labor under very stressful deadlines. Long hours are spent sketching patterns, cutting cloth, sewing, and dyeing. And the judges can be unforgiving when the garments are seen on the runway—much like buyers and fashion magazine editors in the real world. As fashion icon Heidi Klum famously said hundreds of times over her sixteen seasons hosting the show, "In fashion, one day you're in. And the next day, you're out."[25]

Despite the fickle nature of the clothing business, fashion designers play a very important role. Americans buy an average of sixty-four items of clothing every year, according to the American Apparel & Footwear Association. Although 98 percent of those garments are made outside the United States, Americans design most of the clothing sold domestically. And while almost everyone has heard of Coco Chanel and Ralph Lauren, most garments sold in stores are designed by people whose names are largely unknown.

Fashion designers create a wide range of clothing for women, men, and children. Mass-produced clothing, known as ready-to-wear, includes sportswear, maternity wear, outerwear, underwear, and formal wear. Some fashion designers specialize in accessories such as hosiery, handbags, scarves, jewelry, belts, eyewear, and footwear.

Whether a fashion designer works as a freelancer or full-time employee for a large company like Old Navy, the work is similar. Fashion designers sketch clothing designs, make patterns, sew, study fashion trends, and are well acquainted with different types of fabrics and garment production. Most fashion designers oversee every aspect of a design, from the initial sketch to manufacturing. They visit fabric producers to select cloth and trim, conduct fittings of prototype garments, and coordinate production of the final product with clothing makers.

The time between creating initial sketches of a garment to seeing it in a clothing store is about eighteen months. Styles change at an incredibly rapid pace. This requires fashion designers to forecast what will be fashionable in the future. Designers predict trends in several ways. They keep an eye on the collections presented on catwalks by major fashion houses. Designers then create similar garments with less expensive materials that can be sold to the public at lower prices. Designers also rely on predictions published by trade industry groups. These trend reports describe what colors, fabrics, and styles will likely be popular in the coming seasons. Fashion journalist José Teunissen tells designers to visit trendy clubs or shopping districts where fashionable young people hang out. "People who observe new trends in the streets and boutiques [can] translate them for the ready-to-wear industry. . . . [This is] known as forecast styling,"[26] he says.

How Do You Become a Fashion Designer?

Education and Training

Most who succeed at fashion design are often obsessed with clothing and styles at an early age. Designer Hannah Amundson says her fashion fascination led her to develop artistic and technical skills before she went to college. "I took all the relevant classes my high school offered—Home Ec, Sewing, and a specific 'Fashion Careers' elective," she recalls, "and I did really well at them and enjoyed the process of dreaming up an idea and then executing it, making something that was unique and showcased my personality."[27]

Fashion designers create a wide range of clothing and accessories for women, men, and children. They sketch designs, make patterns, sew, study fashion trends, and learn about different types of fabrics and production methods.

Some successful designers have little or no college education. But most entry-level fashion jobs require an applicant to have a bachelor of fine arts degree in fashion. High school students hoping to get into a fashion school should assemble a portfolio that displays their designs. A fashion designer portfolio contains what are called fashion flats. These are pen and ink illustrations of clothing pieces created by the designer. Another element of a portfolio is called a fashion presentation board. This contains three to six collections. Each collection starts off with an inspiration page collage. This is a grouping of images and fabric swatches that demonstrate the mood and color story of the collection. Photos in the collection need to be high quality. Hiring models and professional photographers can be expensive, but some barter or trade garments in exchange for their services.

Those who attend a fashion institute perfect their sewing, drawing, and patternmaking skills and learn about fashion history, trends, textiles, patterns, and colors. Classes also cover clothing business economics, contracts, picking business partners, and running ad campaigns. At some fashion institutes, successful designers work directly with graduate students.

Skills and Personality

Fashion designers present their artistic visions through words, hand-drawn illustrations, and the garments they produce. Most garments first come to life on a sketchpad or tablet computer, and this provides a blueprint for the designer to create a pattern. Most designers have good computer skills and a knowledge of computer-aided design software like Adobe Illustrator or the free, open-source software Valentina. Good sewing skills are an obvious requirement for designers who cut pieces of cloth and assemble them into garments. Designers rely on good communication skills when working with tailors, sewers, and clothing manufacturers. Sales skills are also important for designers to present their collections to buyers, celebrities, and the public.

On the Job

Employers

The Bureau of Labor Statistics (BLS) says around one-third of fashion designers work for apparel companies like Abercrombie & Fitch, American Eagle, URBN, and Gap. Around 8 percent of fashion designers work for wholesale apparel and accessory manufacturers that sell to retail outlets. Designers in retail and wholesale might work in teams with marketing and advertising people, photographers, models, and creative directors. The BLS says 3 percent of designers work in the motion picture industry creating costumes for actors in films and TV shows.

Around 10 percent of fashion designers are freelancers. And as freelance designer Kristen Anderson says, "Contrary to what every episode of *Project Runway* makes you believe, most fashion designers don't sit around all day hand sketching and draping fabric over

Inspiration and Celebration

"My goal as a designer is to create visual experiences that evoke joy and empower self-expression. I believe dressing up can be a powerful tool for embracing confidence and celebrating individuality, allowing wearers to let the clothes speak for them and evoke a sense of excitement in embracing their true selves. Similar to the allure of discovering a hidden gem, I aspire for my creations—like the coverall bodysuits—to be that unexpected delight for those who encounter them."

—Yitao Li, fashion designer

Quoted in Kristen Bateman, "12 Emerging Designers to Know from the Fall 2024 Fashion Season," *Harper's Bazaar*, March 11, 2024. www.harpersbazaar.com.

dress forms."[28] Designers spend long hours promoting themselves on social media, phoning new clients, overseeing clothing production, and marketing their fashions on e-commerce sites. They also spend time keeping track of business expenses and taxes owed.

Working Conditions

The hours of fashion designers can be long and irregular. Freelancers might work at home but spend time traveling to runway shows, clothing production facilities, and fabric shops. The work can be stressful; rejection is part of the job for freelancers. Those who work in retail or wholesale say the job of designing clothing for the consumer market can be boring and lacks creativity.

Earnings and Advancement

The BLS says the median annual wage for fashion designers in 2023 was $79,290. Those who worked in the motion picture and video industries earned $98,740. Designers who worked in the wholesale apparel industry had a median income of $77,770 in 2023.

Working Hard Behind the Scenes

"Keep in mind that fashion is not all glitz and glam. It requires technical knowledge too. You'll have to learn different body proportions, how to apply measurements, pattern making, uses for different fabrics, etc. . . . It can be hard work to make yourself stand out in a very saturated market. But if you find what makes you unique and stay consistent you may find it rewarding. My favorite moment is seeing my work on a runway or in a magazine and knowing all of the behind the scenes work it took to make it!"

—Sierra Sims, fashion designer

Quoted in Career Village, "Why Did You Choose to Be a Fashion Designer? What Made You Choose That Job?," February 24, 2024. www.careervillage.org.

What Is the Future Outlook for Fashion Designers?

According to the BLS, employment of fashion designers is expected to grow by 5 percent through 2033, slightly more than the average for all occupations. With the rapid change in fashion trends, accelerated by social media influencers, those who choose a career in fashion design can expect to find steady employment.

Find Out More

Council of Fashion Designers of America (CFDA)

https://cfda.com

The CFDA is a trade organization made up of womenswear, menswear, jewelry, and accessory designers. The council offers scholarships, educational and professional programs, and resources and tools for fashion designers.

Fashion Group International (FGI)

www.fgi.org

The FGI is a prominent organization founded nearly one hundred years ago by prominent women in the fashion business. The group holds fashion events nationwide, offers student grants and awards, and publishes an annual fashion report.

Underfashion Club

https://underfashionclub.org

This organization, with a mission to support education and new talent, is made up of professionals in the intimate apparel and underwear business. The website features information about internships, scholarships, trends, and runway shows.

What Does a Creative Director Do?

The crocodile emblem on Lacoste polo shirts is one of the most instantly identifiable logos in the fashion world. Crocodiles have nothing to do with sportswear, but the green-and-red emblem has been credited with helping Lacoste grow from a small tennis shirt producer in 1933 to a modern brand associated with luxury sportwear and fashion. This transformation was driven by creative directors who for decades have used the crocodile logo in Lacoste ad campaigns to shape the public's perception of the brand. Blogger Emily Harper writes:

> The crocodile logo . . . automatically makes customers [recognize] the brand no sooner than they spot a crocodile embroidered on fabric. The crocodile is an animal with a strong personality. It's cooler to sport a crocodile on your clothing than a pelican or a llama. People love animals and relate animals to dif-

At a Glance

Number of Jobs
126,600*

Pay
$117,439 in 2024*

Educational Requirements
Bachelor's degree in fine art, design, fashion, or communications technology

Personal Qualities
Artistic, knowledge of fashion and culture, good communication skills, business acumen

Working Conditions
Full time in offices, studios, and at fashion events; occasional long hours and tight deadlines

Future Job Outlook
Growth of 5 percent through 2033*

* For all art directors

ferent personalities. The assertive nature of the crocodile, especially the one on the Lacoste logo, represents the brand's focus on values like tenacity and elegance.[29]

Logos are one element creative directors use to shape and develop a brand's image. In the fashion industry, creative directors, also referred to as art directors, oversee choosing logo designs, themes, color palettes, and styling. They research fashion trends and sales data to predict colors and styles consumers are most likely to buy. They work with fashion designers, sales teams, marketing managers, and chief executive officers. Some creative directors specialize in clothing, while others focus on accessories. Large companies might have a team of creative directors who oversee various aspects of brand management.

While performing many duties, the central role of a creative director is to communicate a brand's image through words and pictures. According to Felipe Oliveira Baptista, creative director for Lacoste, Kenzo, and other fashion giants, "How you communicate visually, how you tell a story and how clear you are as a storyteller is your biggest strength"[30] as a creative director.

Those who want to tell good stories about fashion brands spend their days studying the creative works of others. Art director Ivan Flugelman says, "Most prolific art directors usually have huge design and art book libraries that become their first point of contact with any project."[31] Creative directors also study fads on social media and take inspiration from the countless digital images found on the internet, including photography websites like Flickr and Google Images.

Those who work as creative directors take inspiration from modern and traditional fashions, literature, fabric design, and cinema. They visit art museums and exhibitions, attend the theater, and even go for long walks to spur their imagination and solve

The crocodile logo features prominently on a Paris billboard promoting the Lacoste fashion brand. Guided by creative directors, advertising campaigns featuring the crocodile logo have helped shape public perception of the brand.

creative problems. "Drink as much culture as you can, and learn," says Baptista. "It's a cliché that knowledge is power, but with creativity it really is, the wider your knowledge is in all the creative fields, the bigger your playground is to create."[32]

Creative directors use their knowledge when selecting surprising or exciting visual elements from a wide palette of cultural influences. The elements are assembled on storyboards, sometimes referred to as mood boards, which are collages of images, text, and materials that capture a theme, a look, or an emotion. Although art and design are central to any creative director's job, these professionals also supervise projects and staff members. Baptista says his mood boards help him explain his vision to creative teams that might include graphic designers, illustrators, photographers, and others. When projects are coming together, the creative director selects the best art, photos, and ad copy. He or she might send the work back for further improvement if necessary. Creative directors also develop budgets and timelines, hire and fire staff, and coordinate project activities with marketers, executives, and other company personnel.

How Do You Become a Creative Director?

Education and Training

Most people do not begin their careers in fashion as creative directors. Growing into the job takes time, experience, and a dedicated interest in art, fashion, people, and culture. High school students who are interested in a career as a creative fashion director should take art, graphics, design, and photography classes. It is also important to have a good working knowledge of art design software like Adobe InDesign, GIMP, and Sketch.

Jamie Mizrahi took a typical path through the fashion world to become the creative director at Juicy Couture USA. Mizrahi worked in clothing stores as a teenager and at fashion magazines after college. Then, Mizrahi says, an unexpected opportunity occurred: "I worked at this place called the Albright Fashion Library that was a place where a [creative director] would come and pull clothes for projects—whether it be commercials, music videos, editorial, [or] celebrity styling. That's kind of how I fell into [the job of creative director]."[33]

Most employers require creative directors to have at least a bachelor's degree in fine art, design, fashion, or communications technology. Students should choose a school accredited by the National Association of Schools of Art and Design, which establishes national standards for undergraduate and graduate degrees in art and design. Institutions like New York University, Parsons School of Design, and the Fashion Institute of Technology are highly respected in the fashion industry.

Fashion school students study studio arts, including drawing, painting, and sculpture. They learn about art history, theory,

Create a Memorable Story

"I don't want to do something just to do something random. I want to be good. I want to take time to really think about it. . . . For me, [a fashion show is about] showing emotion, not clothes, to people who come to see the collection. Also, I know that people . . . see so many shows and you want to feel like you've seen something more than just clothes at the end. When I do that, for me, music, scenography, casting the models—I think you have to do all of that so that when you leave one of my shows you feel like you saw a full story."

—Anthony Vaccarello, creative director at Yves Saint Laurent

Quoted in Derek Blasberg, "Fashion and Art: Anthony Vaccarello," *Gagosian Quarterly*, Fall 2023. https://gagosian.com/quarterly.

and criticism while taking designer courses in digital imaging, typography, and graphic design. General education courses include math, English, and the social sciences. Those who go on to pursue a master's degree in business administration or marketing have an employment and earnings advantage over others in the field.

Fashion firms expect creative directors to have at least five years of previous experience in art- and fashion-related occupations. For this reason, creative directors often begin their careers as graphic illustrators, fashion designers, fashion photographers, fine artists, or other art and design professionals. Working in these positions allows a prospective creative director to build a portfolio with projects that demonstrate skill levels.

Good networking skills are useful for hopeful creative directors seeking job opportunities and career advancement. Those who attend fashion shows and industry events and join professional organizations can ask for recommendations and referrals.

Skills and Personality

Art director Jenny Theolin calls people in her profession "creative polymaths."[34] This term describes those who have a wide-ranging knowledge of art, sculpture, illustration, photography, typestyles, advertising, and consumer psychology. These interests help guide creative directors, who work as team leaders in collaboration with designers, stylists, and other artistic professionals.

Creative directors need good communication skills to manage projects. In addition to speaking and writing clearly, they need to be able to listen and learn from others on their team. Leadership and management qualities are also needed when supervising employees and motivating them to create their best work.

Computer skills are required to work with the latest software used in layout, photography, and design. Business acumen is important for creative directors, who need to understand marketing trends, consumer behavior, brand promotions, and other business aspects of the fashion industry. Creative directors also rely on good organizational skills to prioritize tasks, strategize with clients, write up budgets, and meet deadlines.

On the Job

Employers

Creative directors are employed in many sectors of the economy, including advertising, publishing, and entertainment. In the fashion industry they work for well-known fashion houses. Creative director Olivier Rousteing, who specializes in social media, helped Balmain become the first French label to attract more than 1 million followers on Instagram. Nicolas Ghesquiére has guided brand promotion and social media strategy for Louis Vuitton and other premier fashion labels. Creative directors are also employed by fashion magazines like *Vogue* and *Glamour*, and they work for less-prestigious brands like Forever 21, Gap, and Ross Dress for Less.

Melding History and Pop Culture

"I love a story. I love the history of a brand. I love hearing about how these design icons or clothes came to exist. I find that really fascinating, but at the same time I also personally love counter-culture, youth culture and the next generation pop culture. I'm a huge fan of pop music, pop art, pop anything. It's that combination, juxtaposition of storytelling and heritage and craft with pop culture, counter-culture—those two things that I love coming together is, ultimately, my design and creative sensibility."

—Stuart Vevers, creative director at Coach

Quoted in Ana Colón, "How Stuart Vevers Went from Making His Own Club Clothes to Shaping the Future of Coach," Fashionista, August 9, 2021. https://fashionista.com.

Working Conditions

Creative directors work full time in offices, in studios, and at fashion events. The work of a creative director in the fashion industry is fast paced and demanding. Hours can be long and unpredictable before and during busy periods like a company's fashion week. Travel is often required. Creative directors need to keep ahead of the latest trends in fashion and the fashion business.

Earnings and Advancement

The job of creative director is considered one of the top professions in the fashion industry, and those who work in this position are well paid. The salary website Zippia says creative directors earned an average annual salary of $117,439 in 2024. The top 10 percent of earners brought in $229,000.

What Is the Future Outlook for Creative Directors?

The Bureau of Labor Statistics (BLS) puts creative fashion directors in the general category of art directors. The BLS says employment for all art directors is expected to grow by 5 percent through 2033. And as long as fashion houses continue to present seasonal clothing lines on a regular basis, those who work as creative directors will have plenty of job opportunities.

Find Out More

AIGA

www.aiga.org

AIGA is the oldest and largest professional graphic design organization. It works to advance design as a professional craft and advocates for a greater understanding of the value of design and designers in government, business, and media.

Art Directors Guild (ADG)

https://adg.org

The ADG is a labor union made up of art directors, graphic artists, illustrators, production designers, and others who work in entertainment and advertising. The guild publishes *Perspective* magazine, hosts annual awards, and provides a jobs board for members.

One Club for Creativity

www.oneclub.org

This international organization of art directors provides an in-depth look into the industry with articles, videos, photo albums, and podcasts. The club champions education with its Young Ones Club for Creativity, student awards ceremony, and scholarships aimed at the next generation of creative directors.

What Does a Fashion Marketing Manager Do?

Viewers might not realize that when they watch popular music videos, they are often seeing extended commercials. Fashion brands such as Prada, Dolce & Gabbana, Nike, Chanel, and others pay huge sums for product placement. This is the practice of paying superstars like Sabrina Carpenter, Chappell Roan, Beyoncé, and Post Malone to display their products in music videos. The reason is simple; 70 percent of consumers say they are more likely to purchase a product after seeing it in a music video, according to the marketing company Hollywood Branded. Product placement is also common in TikTok videos, TV shows, podcasts, and movies.

At a Glance

Number of Jobs
22,200 in 2023*

Pay
$156,580 in 2023*

Educational Requirements
Bachelor's degree in marketing, fashion communications, or business

Personal Qualities
Creative, analytical, good tech skills, good communication skills

Working Conditions
Full time in a high-pressure industry with occasional long hours and tight deadlines

Future Job Outlook
Growth of 8 percent through 2033*

* For all advertising, promotions, and marketing managers

Getting products in front of consumer eyeballs is just one of the many tasks performed by fashion marketing managers, sometimes known as chief marketing officers (CMOs). These professionals meld creative vision with business acumen to promote clothing and accessories to targeted audiences. They analyze fashion trends, consumer behavior, and sales statistics to determine the best ways to promote their companies, drive brand awareness, and boost sales.

Every year in the United States, the fashion industry spends around half a billion dollars on advertising, according to the data website Statista. And fashion marketing managers are at the epicenter of this massive advertising bonanza. They create brand marketing campaigns for e-commerce, social media, print media, television, sports events, and runway shows. The work includes estimating demand for a product, identifying potential new markets, organizing celebrity and influencer sponsorships, and overseeing marketing teams. Savage x Fenty CMO Natalie Guzman says her job is to stay on top of the marketplace. She asserts, "We look across seasons at what [features] resonate and what causes things to sell out really fast. That helps us understand what drives demand and what to lean into. . . . And there are so many places to [reach customers]. You've got influencers, e-commerce, physical retail, social media. Right now, innovating in these spaces matters more than ever."[35]

Fashion marketing managers determine ad budgets. They negotiate contracts with influencers, celebrities, magazines and newspapers, and entertainment companies. Some marketing managers work with advertising agencies that create and implement product campaigns. Sometimes companies produce ad campaigns in-house. In these situations the fashion marketing manager oversees photo and video shoots and supervises copywriters, graphic artists, and others who create ads. In addition to running ad campaigns, fashion marketing managers use their expertise to determine what a product will cost in a store. To maximize profits, they devise purchasing incentives such as rebates and sales.

Fashion marketing managers might be specialists. Some fashion marketing managers work as visual merchandisers in retail stores. Fashion marketer Anastasia Nicole explains, "Visual merchandisers are responsible for the look and feel of a store.

You are trying to balance the creativity of showcasing the latest trends with making sure you're driving the business by making the store easy to shop."[36] In this role, visual merchandisers create window displays, design store layouts, and display goods to attract customers into stores.

Social media marketing managers focus on promoting their fashion brands on platforms like Facebook, TikTok, and Instagram. They create engaging content and interact with online communities.

Fashion marketing managers rely on programs like Google Analytics to analyze engagement metrics and determine how well their marketing strategies are working. Analytics are also the central focus of fashion marketing managers who work in e-commerce. These marketers study sales data and use it to make decisions about product placement on a company's website and to create markdowns and sales specials. E-commerce specialists are required to sort through consumer comments and complaints to optimize the shopping experience.

How Do You Become a Fashion Marketing Manager?

Education and Training

Most fashion marketing managers have a bachelor's degree in marketing, fashion merchandising, communications, or a related field. But as with many highly desirable jobs in fashion, most who work in this profession have years of experience in other areas of the industry. Some start as associates on the retail floor; others take related jobs as sales representatives, market research analysts, or public relations specialists.

Freelancers can launch their careers at home. Chrissy Chandler's success as a fashion marketing manager provides a good example. Chandler began her fashion marketing career in 2006, selling lingerie on eBay from an office in her garage. She built

Connecting with Customers

"[My biggest priority at Revolve is] making sure that our brand stays relevant and competitive, not just in the US, but globally. . . . How do we get better? How do we continue to engage with our current customer base and also acquire new ones? It's something I obsess about—how to connect with them, be it through social media, events, press, etc. And also thinking about the product and site experience. Ultimately, the customer dictates exactly what she wants. And so I just try to be super mindful of what they are looking for, to make sure that we are relevant and top of mind for them."

—Raissa Gerona, chief brand officer at Revolve

Quoted in Jeffrey Yan, "Raissa Gerona of Revolve on What It Takes to Build a Billion-Dollar Brand," *Harper's Bazaar*, January 24, 2024. www.harpersbazaar.com.

her brand on social media, posting a steady stream of attractive content. Chandler eventually gained over 250,000 followers to her Instagram account, which helped her attract hundreds of thousands of customers, including influencers, entertainers, and performers. In 2012 Chandler founded the online fashion brand Amazing Lace, which is now a multimillion-dollar company.

Most fashion marketing managers do not start their own companies, but the job has great potential for advancement. High school students interested in a career in fashion marketing can begin by conducting research into the sales practices of their favorite brands. Study the websites, social media feeds, and other content produced by leading fashion brands. Blogger Ana M. Marcos offers this advice: "Notice or study all of the marketing strategies they use to interact with their audience/customers, from in-person to digital marketing. See if you can interview or shadow someone with a Fashion Marketing career."[37] Marcos suggests

Fashion marketing managers combine creative vision with business acumen to drive brand awareness and boost sales. To do this they analyze fashion trends, sales statistics, and how people shop.

checking out job listings for fashion marketing managers on sites like Glassdoor to see what companies require in terms of education and experience.

Internships

Those who attend a university or fashion institute will have an opportunity to work as an intern at a fashion company. Internships provide students with hands-on experience and help them develop skills that will lead to better employment opportunities and higher salaries. Emily Ocasio was a University of Connecticut student majoring in communications and marketing in 2023 when she became a fashion intern. Ocasio says she quickly learned that the fashion business is not as glamorous as it looks to outsiders. Much of the hard work is done by interns, who plan runway events and clean up afterward. But she says her internship helped her network with designers, models, photographers, and magazine writers who provided valuable advice and industry contacts. Ocasio concludes, "Overall, being a fashion intern is without a doubt a great experience to have, especially for those who want a future in the industry. You will meet a lot of amazing people and have opportunities to dress up."[38]

Skills and Personality

Fashion marketing managers are skilled analysts who predict consumer buying habits, evaluate industry trends, develop strategies to promote new products, and devise targeted marketing campaigns. To achieve the best results, fashion marketers need good technical skills to navigate the internet and social media platforms. They use tools and software that allow them to analyze website data, click-through rates, and other social media engagement metrics. This requires fashion marketing managers to understand Google Analytics, the Hootsuite social media management platform, content management system software, project management software such as Asana and Trello, and search engine optimization tools like Semrush. Marketing expert Justin Paulsen explains the importance of data and analytics for fashion marketing managers: "Online marketplaces often speak to huge numbers of prospective customers at once. This means that measuring the [effectiveness] of a given piece of [ad] content will require the ability to play with numbers and data to discern patterns and trends. In short, the . . . marketer must be comfortable with statistics."[39]

Leadership skills are also important for fashion marketing managers, since many oversee large sales and production teams. Good leaders communicate clearly and persuasively when running meetings, managing people of various skill levels, and diplomatically explaining complex issues to others.

Fashion marketing managers draw on their creative instincts when generating innovative new ideas for advertising campaigns. Since campaigns have many moving parts, marketing managers need organizational skills to manage personnel, budgets, and time frames.

A Mission and a Message

"In a fashion environment where the offering is humongous, marketing is the only way to stand out to customers. Marketing today is no longer about communicating the right product at the right moment; it is having a mission and proving the brand identity through compelling storytelling. It's about creating a community of people (ultimately customers) that follow your brand with a sense of belonging. Moreover, for fashion brands in a digital era, marketing needs to be always more the flywheel of big social messages, such as sustainability, diversity, inclusivity and tech innovation."

—Anna Moro, global head of marketing and communication at La DoubleJ

Quoted in Federica Pantanella, "A Day in the Life of a Marketing Director with Anna Moro," Beyond Talent, February 22, 2021. https://beyondtalentrecruitment.com.

On the Job

Employers

Fashion marketing managers work for fashion brands, clothing stores and boutiques, and businesses that manufacture clothing and accessories. Some open their own fashion marketing agencies and oversee a staff that produces ad campaigns from start to finish.

Working Conditions

Fashion marketing managers work full time with overtime during Fashion Week, winter holidays, and other busy times for retailers. They spend a lot of time communicating with others on the phone or by emails, texts, letters, and memos. The fashion industry is a high-pressure environment and can be stressful as deadlines loom.

Earnings and Advancement

The Bureau of Labor Statistics (BLS) does not have a separate category for fashion marketing managers. The BLS says the median annual earnings for all advertising, promotions, and marketing managers in 2023 was $156,580.

What Is the Future Outlook for Fashion Marketing Managers?

Employment for advertising, promotions, and marketing managers is expected to grow by 8 percent through 2033. Demand for these professionals is expected to expand as more fashion companies seek to expand their global market share among a new generation of online shoppers.

Find Out More

American Association of Advertising Agencies (4A's)

www.aaaa.org

Known as the 4A's, this organization provides comprehensive information about advertising and business development. The Learning Institute section on its website offers workshops, certification, leadership training, and educational courses.

American Marketing Association (AMA)

www.ama.org

The AMA provides education and certification for future marketers and professionals already working in the field. Its website offers members guidebooks and academic journals, a job board, educational videos, and webinars.

United States Fashion Industry Association (USFIA)

www.usfashionindustry.com

The USFIA is a trade group made up of brands, retailers, importers, and wholesale producers. The group hosts webinars, produces reports on global trade, and stages events.

Introduction: Fashioning a Career

1. Quoted in Oprah.com "American Icon Ralph Lauren and His Family," May 18, 2011. www.oprah.com.
2. Janet Francis, "What Type of Jobs Are in the Fashion Industry?," Career Village, August 23, 2023. www.careervillage.org.
3. Quoted in Nicolas Vega, "Billionaire Tory Burch Says This Is the No. 1 Reason She's Successful: 'I Can't Believe I'm Still Standing,'" CNBC, April 25, 2024. www.cnbc.com.

Fashion Photographer

4. Mark Delong, "What It Takes to Create a Full Fashion Story," Mark Delong Photography, 2024. www.markdelong.com.
5. Quoted in Piscart, "Pro Kait Robinson Tells Stories Through Fashion Photography," 2024. https://picsart.com.
6. Quoted in Piscart, "Pro Kait Robinson Tells Stories Through Fashion Photography."
7. Allen Harper, "How to Use Hashtags on Instagram Properly as a Photographer," PetaPixel, June 22, 2016. https://petapixel.com.
8. Nick Harington, "Exploring the Impact of Photography on the Fashion Industry," Portfoliobox, April 11, 2024. www.portfoliobox.net.

Fashion Stylist

9. Quoted in Janelle Sessoms, "How Zadrian Smith Went from Trained Dancer to A-List Celebrity Stylist," Fashionista, February 7, 2024. https://fashionista.com.
10. Quoted in Kristen Wagner, "Get to Know Kate Young, the Legendary Celebrity Stylist from Easton," Lehigh Valley Style, August 21, 2023. https://lehighvalleystyle.com.
11. Quoted in Yasmin Gagne, "'I Only Put Her in Things Other People Had Worn': Law Roach on His Zendaya Styling Strategy," *Fast Company*, October 26, 2024. www.fastcompany.com.

12. Quoted in Valerie Tejeda, "How to Become a Stylist: Career Tips from a Celebrity Stylist," *Teen Vogue*, February 2, 2018. www.teenvogue.com.
13. Quoted in Tejeda, "How to Become a Stylist."
14. Kristen Swain, "Hazards of Being a Fashion Stylist," Chron, 2024. https://work.chron.com.
15. Swain, "Hazards of Being a Fashion Stylist."

Retail Buyer

16. Katie Guest, "Want to Become a Top Fashion Buyer?," Fashion and the Free, 2023. www.fashionandthefree.com.
17. Ariane, "My Not So Glamorous Life as a Fashion Buyer," Rue Madame, 2022. https://ruemadame.com.
18. Ariane, "My Not So Glamorous Life as a Fashion Buyer."
19. Ivonne, "A Day in the Life: What a Fashion Buyer Actually Does," Fashion Mentor, 2023. www.fashionmentor.co.
20. Ivonne, "A Day in the Life."
21. Quoted in Faves, "When Art Meets Science: The Top Skills of a Fashion Buyer," 2024. https://thefavesapp.com.
22. Karen Lott, Vault, "A Day in the Life: Fashion Buyer (Fabric)," April 15, 2021. https://vault.com.
23. Ariane, "My Not So Glamorous Life as a Fashion Buyer."

Fashion Designer

24. Quoted in Kristen Bateman, "12 Emerging Designers to Know from the Fall 2024 Fashion Season," *Harper's Bazaar*, March 11, 2024. www.harpersbazaar.com.
25. Quoted in Jane Lewis, "Fashion on Fifth: You're Either In or You're Out," *New School Free Press*, February 16, 2024. www.newschoolfreepress.com.
26. Quoted in Esmee Blaazer, "How Do You Predict Fashion?," Fashion United, January 1, 2024. https://fashionunited.com.
27. Quoted in Career Village, "Why Did You Choose to Be a Fashion Designer? What Made You Choose That Job?," February 24, 2024. www.careervillage.org.
28. Kristen Anderson, "A Day in the Life of a Fashion Designer," krstn ndrsn design studio, March 24, 2023. www.kndrsn.com.

Creative Director

29. Emily Harper, "The Lacoste Logo & Brand: Serendipity Meets Great Branding," LOGO, May 23, 2023. https://logo.com.
30. Quoted in Polimoda, "The Wider Your Knowledge, the Bigger Your Playground," August 5, 2024. www.polimoda.com.
31. Ivan Flugelman, "How to Become a Better Art Director," Medium, July 27, 2016. https://ivanflugelman.medium.com.
32. Quoted in Polimoda, "The Wider Your Knowledge, the Bigger Your Playground."
33. Quoted in Madeline Hill, "How Celebrity Stylist Jamie Mizrahi Landed Her Big Break," Who What Wear, April 17, 2024. www.whowhatwear.com.
34. Quoted in Nare Navasardyan, "How to Become an Art Director," Piscart, 2024. https://picsart.com.

Fashion Marketing Manager

35. Quoted in Danny Parisi, "Savage x Fenty Co-president & CMO Natalie Guzman: 2022 Top Marketer," Glossy, June 1, 2022. www.glossy.co.
36. Quoted in Melanie, "What Could You Do with a Fashion Marketing Degree?," Career Village, December 22, 2023. www.careervillage.org.
37. Quoted in London, "If I Have a Degree in Fashion Marketing What Are the Different Job Options and What Do They Do?," Career Village, August 6, 2024. www.careervillage.org.
38. Emily Ocasio, "My Experience as a Fashion Intern," Her Campus, 2024. www.hercampus.com.
39. Justin Paulsen, "How to Become a Content Marketing Manager," Tech Guide, May 13, 2024. https://techguide.org.

Jay Marroquin has worked as a photographer for twenty years, with a focus on fashion photography for the past fifteen years. He answered these questions in a telephone interview. Comments have been edited for length and clarity.

Q: Why did you become fashion photographer?

A: I don't have a romantic story where I say, "Oh my parents passed me down this camera." When I was eighteen, I went to New York City, and that's when I decided to take photos. I came away with it by working with an established hairstylist. He opened some doors for me in New York and really taught me what it was to actually take a fashion photo. I wanted to do an art exhibit, and he offered his services as a hairstylist. Once you start working with somebody like a hairstylist, you realize, whoa, there's makeup, there's wardrobe, there's so many aspects of it. And that opened so many doors in New York including working behind the scenes during Fashion Week.

Q: Can you describe your typical workday?

A: I spend a lot of time working on the business side of things, reaching out to clients, talking to them, and putting together mood boards for them. It's much more than just the photographs. I probably work bigger shoots around two or three times a month, and each of those requires three or four days of planning with wardrobe and different team members. So, a typical workday is going through the real grind of work: emails, putting the schedule together, what needs to be done for the photo shoot. It's really all the work that goes into it before you take a single photo.

Q: What do you like most about your job?

A: The interactions with people. I like meeting with people and having the creativity to bring out something that's my vision. And I enjoy meeting a client's expectations and exceeding them at times.

Q: What do you like least about your job?

A: I'm based in Houston. You have to know your market, and you have to know your work. In Houston there's just not the biggest budgets for fashion work, and you have to be realistic with what's required for that. What I like least is sometimes it requires a bigger budget than what people think. And you have to know how to sell them on it. And sometimes clients unfortunately do not have realistic expectations about what it takes to put together the shot they want with the mood board and the inspirations they have. It's not fun to let them know "You really can't do that with your budget."

Q: What personal qualities do you find most valuable for this type of work?

A: You have to be a social butterfly; you can't be an introverted person. You have to able to talk to people. And if you really want to do this as a business and have this be your career, you have to know your work so you can sell yourself. You have to have the ability to believe in yourself, and you have to be a salesperson. And then you have to be an artist and be able to create.

Q: What advice do you have for students who might be interested in this career?

A: Do your research. Spend time reading some books. Take your time; there's more to it than just going out and photographing things. Shoot as often as possible. Learn about your craft.

Q: What types of projects are you currently working on?

A: One project I call "Encounters," which documents my random encounters with strangers. I say to them, "If I ask to photograph you, it's because you're beautiful." This statement rings true. I think people's imperfections are exactly what make them beautiful. In a world where we're bombarded by other people's definition of beauty or an unrealistic expectation, I'd like for people to realize they indeed are beautiful just the way they are. Most if not all the ads you see are not a true reflection of people. A ton of Photoshop and retouching goes into those photos and ads. I don't want my daughter to grow up in a world that sees flawless skin as beautiful. There's nothing wrong with that; just don't make that the definition of beauty for those that don't have flawless skin or a perfectly symmetrical face. I prefer using a trusty Nikon 35mm camera and the look of grainy film for this project. The close-up proximity of the camera to the face also makes it rather intimate. To date I've probably captured over five hundred faces all around the world.

Other Jobs in the Fashion Industry

Accessory designer
Advertising sales agent
Convention planner
Copywriter
Craft artist
Customer service representative
Display designer
Dyeing supervisor
Fashion illustrator
Fashion writer
Film and video editor
Floral designer
Graphic designer
Jeweler
Knitting machine technician
Lighting technician
Market research analyst
Model
Patternmaker
Public relations specialist
Retail interior designer
Retail sales worker
Screen printer
Shoe designer
Social media manager
Tailor
Textile production manager
Videographer
Weaver
Wholesale and manufacturing sales representative

Editor's note: The online *Occupational Outlook Handbook* of the US Department of Labor's Bureau of Labor Statistics is an excellent source of information on jobs in hundreds of career fields, including many of those listed here. The *Occupational Outlook Handbook* may be accessed online at www.bls.gov/ooh.

Index

Note: Boldface page numbers indicate illustrations.

Cover: Dragon Images/Shutterstock

11: Gorodenkoff/Shutterstock
16: DFree/Shutterstock
33: PeopleImages.com-Yuri A/Shutterstock
40: HUBC/Shutterstock
50: Q88/Shutterstock

About the Author

Stuart A. Kallen is the author of more than 350 nonfiction books for children and young adults. He has written on topics ranging from the theory of relativity to the art of electronic dance music. Kallen won a Green Earth Book Award from the Nature Generation environmental organization for his book *Trashing the Planet: Examining the Global Garbage Glut*. In his spare time he is a singer, songwriter, and guitarist in San Diego.